Akashic U.S. Presidents Series

NEAL POLLACK on JOHN ADAMS

Akashic U.S. Presidents Series

NEAL POLLACK on JOHN ADAMS

A Defence of the Constitutions of Government of the United States of America

Akashic Books
New York

AKASHIC BOOKS PRESENTS a thought-provoking series of early writings from United States Presidents, starting with George Washington and moving chronologically forward to John Adams (in this volume), Thomas Jefferson, and beyond. Each slim book offers an introduction by a groundbreaking contemporary writer. This series is unlike any other Presidential commentaries in print, and is characterized by a critical viewpoint that will provide a counterpoint to the more staid analyses that have traditionally accompanied Presidential writings.

The bust of John Adams on the cover of this book was sculpted in 1818 by French artist M.J. Binon and installed in Boston's Faneuil Hall, where it still stands.

Published by Akashic Books
Introduction ©2004 Neal Pollack

ISBN: 1-888451-61-0
Library of Congress Control Number: 2004106237
Printed in Canada
First printing

Akashic Books
PO Box 1456
New York, NY 10009
Akashic7@aol.com
www.akashicbooks.com

Contents

Introduction

Upon John Quincy Adams's commencement of studies where all future Presidents get their start—at the University of Leyden, in Holland—his father, John Adams, gave him some advice. According to David McCullough's Adams biography, your one-stop shopping source for all things John Adams, it was a paternal imperative that John Quincy attend all lectures possible in law, medicine, chemistry, and philosophy. As a starter kit, Adams the elder sent his son several volumes of Alexander Pope and an edition of Terence, his favorite Roman author, in both Latin and French, saying that

Terence is "remarkable, for good morals, good taste, and good Latin . . . His language has simplicity and elegance that make him proper to be accurately studied as a model."

For those parents among us who think they're educating their children well, I offer the relationship of John Adams and John Quincy Adams as comparison. We should all hide our Montessori blocks, after-school French lessons, and Boy's State scholarship applications in shame. And multiply by ten everything you've read, since many 18th-century universities presented their lectures exclusively in Latin. John Quincy Adams went to college, in a foreign country, at age thirteen.

Imagine John Adams's rage, then, when horror of horrors, he discovered that his son's course of study didn't include Cicero and Demosthenes. He insisted that John Quincy begin an independent course of study at once, while also encouraging him to learn the "fine arts" of ice-skating, riding, fencing, and dancing. "Everything in life should be done with reflection," said the wise father. And he had some more practical New England advice:

> Read somewhat in the English poets every day. You will find them elegant, entertaining, and constructive companions through your whole life . . . You will never be alone with a poet in your pocket. You will never have an idle hour.

Given the hygiene and general manners of my poetic acquaintances, I find the idea of a poet in my pocket quite unappealing. But Adams's sentiment is eternal and untouchable. What possible equivalent, in today's educationally diminished age of standardized testing, forged term papers, and ideologically charged culture wars, could there possibly be? "Son, the sum total of a man is his performance on the AP Geography exam." "You should major in something useful, like Economics or Business." "The literary canon is the product of centuries of white male patriarchy. Read Maxine Hong Kingston and Alice Walker instead." The *gravitas* just isn't there.

"You will ever remember," said John Adams in a letter to his young son, "that all the end of study

11

is to make you a good man and a useful citizen." I hope someone can immediately produce forensic evidence to prove me wrong, but it seems unlikely that letters like that get written anymore.

John Adams (elder) was born the son of a commonplace New England farmer, to a family of values so straightforward and simple that, as an Adams family member wrote, "A hat would descend from father to son, and for fifty years make its regular appearance at a meeting." Yet stinky hat notwithstanding, Adams rose to the heights of history, and he did so in large part because of his education.

Forgive my potted history of the Enlightenment here, but I shall do my best. The second half of the 1700s was a golden time when most intellectuals shared the belief that the power of reason could lead to human perfectibility. Observation and experience became the building blocks for moral values, scientific inquiry, and the construction of nation-states. The Bible and Greek philosophy were to be studied, but not followed as dogma, and the religious trend of the day was Deism, a belief in an all-seeing God. Theology was anathema, and the "Church," in all its forms, the root of evil, since it corrupted the free exercise of reason.

Those were the days of Voltaire and Franklin, Jefferson and Diderot, Locke and Hume, and a wild all-night club scene. The Enlightenment was cosmopolitan and antinationalistic. The publication of books and newspapers, combined with changes in technology, exploded under Enlightenment influence. It became fashionable, and, I'm sure, hilarious, for the upper classes to perform scientific experiments of their own at home. While the era waned, for good reason, after Marie Antoinette's head hit the ground in the Bastille, its influence paved the way for modern political and economic liberalism, humanitarian reform, and a belief in the necessity of progress. Then there was a little thing called the American Revolution.

I'm not the first, or even the 8,000th person to say that our Founding Fathers forged the Revolution through Enlightenment ideals and established the nation while adhering to those ideals with remarkable consistency. America as they conceived it would be the ultimate laboratory of human perfectibility, with reasoned knowledge the key to citizenship in this glowing country on the hill. At this point, I'm sure you see that this essay can't possibly reach a happy conclusion. But allow me to talk about John Adams a little more before we get to the depressing bits.

Throughout his public career, Adams was dogged by the accusation that he was, in his heart, a secret monarchist. There's much empirical evidence, some of it from the practical New England workhorse's mouth, to show this as the truth. Adams, while on a seemingly endless diplomatic mission to France, found himself entranced by Paris under the Sun King, and he expressed little but revulsion at the Jacobins who overthrew him. He believed that Americans had the right to self-govern, but could never bring himself to hate George III, or even blame the excesses of colonial rule on him. He also, it should be remembered, defended the British soldiers who perpetrated the Boston Massacre, not only because he felt they had a right to fair trial, but also because he believed the mob was equally at fault. John Adams was no friend of the mythical *common man.*

Thus we arrive at John Adams's *A Defence of the Constitutions of Government of the United States of America,* several vital excerpts of which are included in this volume. Adams's 1787 *Defence* was a rebuttal to French economist Turgot's critique of the direction of the budding American government. Penned just as the American experiment began to take physical form, Adams here makes his most important contribution to our system of government. He proposes a bicameral legislature, and does so, I might add, at considerable cost to his personal and political reputation. His "defence" concedes, as few politicians then could or now can, that society, by its very nature, creates class differences:

> Wherever we have seen a territory somewhat larger, arts and sciences more cultivated, commerce flourishing, or even agriculture improved to any great degree, an aristocracy has risen up in a course of time, con-

sisting of a few rich and honourable families, who have united with each other against both the people and the first magistrate; who have wrested from the former, by art and by force, all their participation in the government; and have even inspired them with so mean an esteem of themselves, and so deep a veneration and strong attachment to their rulers, as to believe and confess them a superior order of beings.

Adams thought that a philosopher king and his philosopher court, a council of wise persons, as it were, should be the true rulers of a free country. It's important to note, too, that he places "art," "science," and "force" in equal stature. Guns alone cannot rule a country, and only knowledge will liberate us from our earthly chains.

But just when you think that Adams is public snob number one, he throws a slider: "Shall we conclude, from these melancholy observations, that human nature is incapable of liberty, that no honest equality can be preserved in society, and that such forcible causes are always at work as must reduce all men to a submission to despotism, monarchy, oligarchy, or aristocracy? By no means."

Adams realized that a land ruled only by the elite would necessarily be shaped to meet the needs of that elite alone. America would be made great not because of its leaders, but because the leaders had established a social framework where citizens were free to own property, where trial by jury was a God-given right, and where a totally free press operated without fear of government reprisal. Still, and here's where Adams could be complicated and exasperating, the aristocracy was better, intrinsically, than the mass. We must be honest, he said:

What are we to understand here by equality? Are the citizens to be all of the same age, sex, size, strength, stature, activity, courage, hardiness, industry, patience, ingenuity, wealth, knowledge, fame, wit, temperance, constancy, and wisdom? Was there, or will there ever be, a nation, whose individuals were all equal, in natural and acquired qualities, in virtues, talents, and riches? The answer of all mankind must be in the negative.— It must then be acknowledged, that in every state, in the Massachusetts, for example, there are inequalities which God and nature have planted there, and which no human legislator ever can eradicate.

If a politician, or even pundit, were to say that in today's America, they'd be rhetorically tarred and feathered. Why, this is America, the land of opportunity, where all men are created equal. We don't like our politicians to be rich, even though most of them are. So we'd rather have them pretend to be "one of us."

Bosh, Adams said:

There is an inequality of wealth; some individuals, whether by descent from their ancestors, or from greater skill, industry, and success in business, have estates both in lands and goods of great value; others have no property at all; and of all the rest of society, much the greater number are possessed of wealth, in all the variety of degrees between these extremes; it will easily be conceived that all the rich men will have many of the poor, in the various trades, manufactures, and other occupations in life, dependent upon them for their daily bread: many of smaller fortunes will be in their debt, and in many ways under obligations to them: others, in better circumstances, neither dependent nor in debt, men of letters, men of the learned professions, and others, from acquaintance, conversation, and civilities, will be connected with them and attached to them.

In other words, four semicolons later, some people are rich, some people are poor, and that's the way of the world. Even more scabrously, Adams dared postulate that not all people are *born* equal. "The children of illustrious families," he wrote,

have generally greater advantages of education, and earlier opportunities to be acquainted with public characters, and informed of public affairs, than those of meaner ones, or even than those in middle life; and what is more than all, an habitual national veneration for their names, and the characters of their ancestors described in history, or coming down by tradition, removes them farther from vulgar jealousy and popular envy, and secures them in some degree the favor, the affection, and respect of the public.

Well, I guess that explains Gore Vidal, but what about those of us who are born a son of a simple farmer, or, say, a mid-level insurance executive, or a failed minor-league baseball player? The answer, as Adams so often wrote, lies in education. "We cannot presume," he says,

that a man is good or bad, merely because his father was one or the other; and we should always inform ourselves first, whether the virtues and talents are inherited, before we yield our confidence. Wise men beget fools, and honest men knaves; but these instances, although they may be frequent, are not general. If there is often a likeness in feature and figure, there is generally more in mind and heart, because education contributes to the formation of these as well as nature.

The idea of equal access to education, to the great intellectual advancements of the

Enlightenment, to reasoned inquiry, is at the core of all Adams's writing, and indeed was the intellectual core of this country's founding. Without it, the specter of tyranny begins to cast its shadow. I quote at length here, for almost the last time:

> We have seen, both by reasoning and in experience, what kind of equality is to be found or expected in the simplest people in the world. There is not a city nor a village, any more than a kingdom or a commonwealth, in Europe or America; not a horde, clan, or tribe, among the negroes of Africa, or the savages of North or South America; nor a private club in the world, in which inequalities are not more or less visible . . . But, as long as human nature shall have passions and imagination, there is too much reason to fear that these advantages, in many instances, will have more influence than reason and equity can justify.

Because of John Adams's reasoned inquiry into the nature of humankind and the nature of human government, we have the separation of the executive branch of government from the legislative, and the separation of the House of Representatives from the Senate. In one chamber, you have the council of wise elders. In the other, officials truly elected from among the people. Through the electoral mechanisms of the House, more people are allowed to join the governing elite. To Adams's mind, though, the diversification of political power is equal, if not secondary, to the fact that new segments of society get to know the pleasures of learning.

THE MOST STRIKING THING about the *Defence*, and about Adams's writing in general, is his extreme sensitivity to moral duty. The state is morally obligated to its citizens, and vice versa. Children are morally obligated to their parents. In fact, Adams even writes that if the Ten Commandments themselves were law, nations would have a "civil right" to repeal them. The one exception to that is the Fifth Commandment. Honoring your father and mother, to Adams, transcends law.

All parents love their children, he says. The "sentiments and affections" of family life "naturally arise." Yet being from a "good" family doesn't necessarily make one a good person. He quotes an "orator" as saying, "I cannot know whether a child of five years old will be a son of liberty or a tyrant."

A high upbringing was important to Adams. In many ways, he was indeed a snob. Almost to a fault, he preferred the company of people of "taste." But he also saw that an aristocracy rots from within. Under a government ruled by *noblesse oblige*, it could be a quick slide from an Octavius to a Caligula. God would bless the leaders of the nation, but the people would choose them. To quote:

> . . . it has pleased the Author of Nature to mingle, from time to time, among the societies of men a few, and but a few of those on whom he has been graciously pleased to confer a larger proportion of the ethereal spirit, than in the ordinary course of his providence he bestows on the sons of men. These are they who engross almost the whole reason of the species. Born to direct, to guide, and to preserve, if they retire from the world their splendor accompanies them, and enlightens even the darkness of their retreat.

If America was to be a special country, these men (Adams could not have forseen Hillary Clinton or . . . I'm trying to think of a powerful Republican woman. It'll come to me. OK. Christine Todd Whitman) would have to be able to come from anywhere. Even Arkansas. Even Plains, Georgia. And I'll throw the other team another bone here: even a small town in Illinois. In Adams's ideal America, greatness would rise from unsuspected places.

Adams also wrote the state Constitution of Massachusetts, and in it included a section, which, as David McCullough writes, "was like no other declaration to be found in any constitution ever written until then, or since." It's called "The Encouragement Of Literature, Etc.," and I ask permission to quote one final time, because I believe no more profound words have ever been written about what America, in its ideal state, should be.

"Wisdom and knowledge," Adams wrote,

as well as virtue, diffused generally among the body of the people being necessary for the preservation of their rights and liberties; and as these depend on spreading the opportunities and advantages of education in various parts of the country, and among the different orders of the people, it shall be the duty of legislators and magistrates in all future periods of this commonwealth to cherish the interests of literature and the sciences, and all seminaries of them, especially the university at Cambridge, public schools, and grammar schools in the towns; to encourage private societies and public institutions, rewards and immunities, for the promotion of agriculture, arts, sciences, commerce, trades, manufactures, and a natural history of the country; to countenance and inculcate the principles of humanity and general benevolence, public and private charity, industry and frugality, honesty and punctuality in their dealings, sincerity, good humor, and all social affections, and generous sentiments among the people.

I fear that today the man who wrote those words is turning uncomfortably in his unmarked grave.

An OUTRAGEOUS STATEMENT: Americans are currently living through the beginning of the age of De-Enlightenment. For those of us who are ostensibly enlightened, this might be difficult to see. History doesn't always move like a rocket. Intellectual changes aren't as easily charted as geopolitical ones. Yet science and reason are beating a retreat into tighter and tighter corners of an increasingly anti-intellectual republic, and are gradually being supplanted by superstition and paranoia masquerading as patriotism. It's gradual, but it's happening. One could even argue, with sufficient evidence, that our current government is waging a quiet war on science and history. If the De-Enlightenment was merely about political corruption in the Bush Administration, it could and will be easily corrected. But the Administration is merely a powerful offshoot of larger forces. Bush will be gone eventually. It won't be so easy to stop the deterioration of the American mind.

I run the danger here of sounding like a paranoid lefty version of Allan Bloom, whose book, *The Closing of the American Mind,* was quite influential in its day nearly twenty years ago, but now seems like a quaint document of a bygone culture war. Bloom's book was largely a conservative ploy to keep African-history seminars out of college curriculums and to stop professors from telling their students that E.M. Forster was gay. If John Adams were alive today, I believe he'd casually ignore gender studies and media studies and four-month courses on the semiotics of *Buffy the Vampire Slayer* and subtly encourage adding the speeches of Nelson Mandela to various reading lists. He'd howl in eternal protest, however, at the roaring tide of fundamentalist religious education that threatens to forever wipe sanity off our national register.

According to an ABC News poll from February 2004, sixty percent of Americans believe that stories in the Bible are literally true, meaning, "It happened that way word for word." Sixty-four percent literally believe that Moses parted the Red Sea. Sixty percent believe that Noah literally loaded an ark with two of every kind of animal in existence before a great flood enveloped the Earth. Most frighteningly, sixty-one percent of Americans believe that God literally created the world in seven days.

How did we get to this place? How did America become a country where more than three out of every five people you sit next to on the bus don't believe in evolution? How did American eighth-graders, in a comprehensive international 1999 study of scientific aptitude, finish nineteenth among all the world's nations, behind such giants of wealth and progress as Slovenia, Bulgaria, and the Russian Federation? Admittedly, we beat Italy, Romania, and Iran, among many others, but that's not exactly a point of pride. Hungary finished third, for heaven's sake!

This poll was taken five years ago. It's almost certain that the numbers have declined since then. In May 2004, the National Science Foundation reported that twenty-four nations in 2000 awarded a higher percentage of science and engineering degrees to students than the United States. The United States awarded 5.7 science degrees per 100 twenty-four-year-olds, compared with a ratio of 13.2 to 100 in Finland, which awarded the highest proportion. Science and reason lose more territory in America every day.

We continue in Cobb County, Georgia, where in September 2002, the school board voted to allow the teaching of "alternative views" about the origin of species in their classrooms. The most prominent "alternative view" is something called "intelligent design," a theory promoted by the Discovery Institute, a Seattle-based nonprofit think tank. On its website, the Institute states that its theories have no basis in creationism or biblical text. But that's fudging the matter a bit. Intelligent designers claim that natural change is the product of a "universal organizing intelligence," rather than, as traditional Darwinists hold, the product of random chance and natural mechanical laws.

All this would add up to an interesting intellectual debate if America wasn't plagued with media-savvy fundamentalists who are willing to use any excuse to insert their doctrine into public discourse. Rather than decry the Cobb County vote, the first sortie in an *Anschluss* of ignorance, the state of Georgia tried to expand the program. In January 2004, the state science commission announced new science teaching guidelines that would omit the word "evolution" entirely. It would now be called "biological changes over time," an unspecific euphemism that could also refer to puberty, or composting. After months of furious debate and protests from Republican and Democratic state legislators alike, the evolutionists carried the day. Georgia adopted a revised science core curriculum that removed all references to "intelligent design" and "alternative" theories of evolution from classroom materials. In addition, five parents have sued the state, demanding that warning stickers about evolution be removed from science textbooks. The warning reads: *"Evolution is a theory, not a fact, regarding the origin of living things. This material should be approached with an open mind, studied carefully and critically considered."* Let's hope they get a sympathetic judge.

But that's just a bunch of ignorant hicks in Georgia, right? Well, in 2004, Ohio's state board of education approved a lesson plan called, "A Critical Analysis of Evolution." In April 2004, the school board in Darby, Montana, voted to require science teachers to assess evidence "for and against" evolution. The Alabama House of Representatives recently expanded its "Academic Freedom Act" to include teachers who wish to cover "scientific information pertaining to the full range of scientific views concerning biological or physical origins." Against the wishes of parents, the school board in Roseville, California, under pressure from a local creationism activist, now allows its libraries to carry anti-evolution books.

This trend reached its highest temperature so far in December 2003, when the Missouri House of Representatives introduced a bill that said, "If scientific theory concerning biological origin is taught, biological evolution and biological intelligent design shall be taught and given equal treatment." It also stipulated that new textbooks abide by requirements of the law, that every classroom in the state must post a copy of the law on the wall, and that "willful neglect of any elementary or secondary school superintendent, principal, or teacher to observe and carry out the requirements of this section shall be cause for termination of his or her contract." In other words, if you teach evolution, you're fired. The bill hasn't passed as of this writing, but someday, somewhere in this country, a bill like it will.

This trend has found its way into national policy. A basically unreported aspect of President George W. Bush's "No Child Left Behind" law is that it specifically encourages schools, through an amendment introduced by Pennsylvania Senator Rick Santorum, to present "a full range of scientific views" on various science topics, "such as biological evolution." To repeat: That language exists in a major federal law in this country, which was founded on the bedrock principle of separation of church and state and on an unshakable belief in science and reason.

Our public schools have been failing for decades, and some very strange ideas are being used to prop them up. The No Child Left Behind

Act has specific provisions calling for "faith-based" education, which is one of the bulwarks of the Bush Presidency. "We've created these offices," Bush said in a July 2003 speech, "whose sole function it is to, one, recognize the power of faith and, two, recognize there are fantastic programs all throughout the country on a variety of subjects, all based upon faith, all changing lives, all making American life better, and therefore, folks would be enlisted in making sure the American dream extends throughout our society."

Warnings about obliterating the separation of church and state aside, few people would be worried if faith-based education merely brought about some after-school math tutoring at neighborhood churches. But there are definitely other agendas at work. In an April 2003 interview with the Baptist Press wire service, which I'm sure he now regrets, Secretary of Education Rod Paige said he believes that children fare better in schools with a "strong appreciation for the values of the Christian community, where a child is taught to have strong faith." He went on to say that "in a religious environment the value system is set. That's not the case in a public school, where there are so many different kids with different kinds of values."

If Rod Paige wants to educate his children in a Christian school with Christian values, that's his right. If he wants to say that Christian schools teach good values, there are many people of all religious backgrounds who'd agree with him. But that's not what he's saying. Our leading public-education official advocates a "set" "value system" that exists in opposition to "public school," which promotes "different kinds of values." This is not a rhetorical slip. This is increasingly the dominant educational doctrine of our time.

The full effect of this trend might not manifest itself for some time. But you can see its "values" starting to seep into all manner of curriculum. Evolution is currently being flogged. We also have federal "abstinence" education, which, among other things, offers cash bonuses to schools that teach "a monogamous relationship within the context of marriage" as the standard of human sexuality and prohibit teaching about contraception.

It gets even more sinister. A high school teacher in Presque Isle, Maine, was recently placed on administrative leave because he protested a new history curriculum that mandated he place emphasis on the evolution of "Christian civilization." The curriculum specifically stated that he wasn't allowed to talk about the influence of Jewish, Islamic, and Asian cultures and religions on the development of European culture. He was also banned from teaching about ancient Greece, which wasn't a "Christian" civilization. Such nonsense has long been *de rigeur* in fundamentalist Christian schools, whose textbooks, according to a study by the group Americans for Religious Liberty, include choice statements like, "The Indian culture typified heathen civilization, lost in darkness without light of the gospel," and, "The Bible does not specifically condemn slavery."

Vile as those sentiments may be, they've typically been applied in private academies, and deserve protection under the U.S. Constitution. Many Christian educational critics argue that our public schools have become mushy with multiculturalism, excessive concern with students' self-esteem, and an unwillingness to teach toward any goal but increasing standardized test scores. They have a point. A John Adams of today would still be appalled that students aren't reading Cicero and Demosthenes. But he'd also be horrified by a textbook called *Biology for Christian Schools*, which instructs: "If the conclusions [of the scientific community] contradict the Word of God, the conclusions are wrong no matter how many scientific facts may appear to back them."

THE DE-ENLIGHTENMENT is occurring in our country. We're being de-enlightened by design, and with little concern for anything other than radical interpretation of biblical prophecy. The anti-evolution Discovery Institute, the home of "intelligent design" theory, is largely funded by Howard Ahmanson, an Orange Country, California, businessman with ties to Christian Reconstruction, an extreme faction of the religious right that seeks to replace American democracy with a harsh fundamentalist theocracy. Christian Reconstructionists regard the teaching of evolution as part of a "war against Genesis." Their version of "biblical law" would sentence to death "adulterers, homosexuals, witches, incorrigible children and those who spread 'false' religions."

Of course, these people are fringe lunatics. The odds that they'll achieve their ideal society is small, to say the least. But the Discovery Institute is making creepy inroads all over the country. Their education plan is called the "Wedge strategy," whose mission statement starts off with relative sanity by stating: "The proposition that human beings are created in the image of God is one of the bedrock principles on which Western civilization was built."

This is a vaguely questionable claim, but hardly out of the bounds of legitimate public discourse. The curriculum goes on to denounce "materialist" intellectuals such as Freud, Marx, and Darwin, who "infected" culture with their ideas that "denied the existence of objective moral standards." These materialist standards, goes the Wedge theory, have created a culture where "everyone is a victim and no one can be held accountable for his or her actions," where a "a virulent strain of utopianism" has created "coercive government programs that falsely promised to create heaven on earth."

The proposal goes from religious conservatism to complete bigoted lunacy in four short paragraphs. The people who drew up this Wedge plan aren't just concerned with broadening our discussion of evolutionary theory. That's just their first block in a master plan to overthrow many aspects of modern society. They've already achieved their "five-year goals" of bringing "design theory" into the public debate. Their "twenty-year goals" are as follows:

• To see intelligent design theory as the dominant perspective in science.

• To see design theory application in specific fields, including molecular biology, biochemistry, paleontology, physics, and cosmology in the natural sciences; psychology, ethics, politics, theology, and philosophy in the humanities; to see its influence in the fine arts.

• To see design theory permeate our religious, cultural, moral, and political life.

That couldn't happen, you say. Not in America. Not in a country where more than sixty percent of the citizens believe the world was created in seven days. Not in a country where the President says he thinks he's in office because God wants him to be. Not in a country where the President has publicly stated that the Bible is a good "rule book" for public policy. No. That could never happen here.

What, I wonder, would John Adams make of all this? If the *Defence* is any guide, I don't think he would blame the people who've come to believe such "unreasonable" ideas. I don't even think he'd blame the people who directly propagate them. Our democracy's skids have always been greased with snake oil. Such are the perils of a free society. The real fault, if I may speak for our second President, lies with the elite. They've grown too comfortable with "natural advantage." There's no real respect for the citizens, no feeling of moral duty. Unchecked inequality festers a society from within. It encourages, even requires, despotism. Only education, true education, can correct the course of tyranny.

Two thousand words ago, I quoted John Adams as saying, "Wisdom and knowledge, as well as virtue, diffused generally among the body of the people" are "necessary for the preservation of their rights and liberties." The goal of such wisdom, he wrote, was "to countenance and inculcate the principles of humanity and general benevolence, public and private charity, industry and frugality, honesty and punctuality in their dealings, sincerity, good humor, and all social affections, and generous sentiments among the people."

Such were the educational philosophies of the Enlightenment. It would serve us well to remember them and teach them to our children, because the odds are increasingly against them learning such principles in school. We no longer live in John Adams's America.

Neal Pollack
Austin, Texas
July 2004

A DEFENCE

OF THE

CONSTITUTIONS

OF GOVERNMENT

OF THE

UNITED STATES

OF AMERICA

[Excerpts from Letters XXIII, XXV, and XXVI]

BY JOHN ADAMS, LL. D

AND A MEMBER OF THE ACADEMY OF ARTS AND SCIENES AT BOSTON.

All nature's difference keeps all nature's peace. POPE.

LETTER XXIII. [excerpt]
RECAPITULATION.

WHEREVER WE HAVE SEEN a territory some-
what larger, arts and sciences more cul-
tivated, commerce flourishing, or even
agriculture improved to any great degree, an aristocracy has risen up in a course of time, consisting
of a few rich and honourable families, who have
united with each other against both the people
and the first magistrate; who have wrested from
the former, by art and by force, all their participation in the government; and have even inspired
them with so mean an esteem of themselves, and
so deep a veneration and strong attachment to
their rulers, as to believe and confess them a superior order of beings.

We have seen these noble families, although necessitated to have a head, extremely jealous of his influence, anxious to reduce his power, and to constrain him to as near a level as possible with themselves; always endeavoring to establish a rotation, by which they may all equally be entitled in turn to the preëminence, and likewise anxious to preserve to themselves as large a share as possible of power in the executive and judicial, as well as the legislative departments of the state.

These patrician families have also appeared in every instance to be equally jealous of each other, and to have contrived, by blending lot and choice, by mixing various bodies in the elections to the same offices, and even by a resort to the horrors of an inquisition, to guard against the sin that so easily besets them, of being wholly influenced and governed by a junto or oligarchy of a few among themselves.

We have seen no one government in which is a distinct separation of the legislative from the executive power, and of the judicial from both, or in which any attempt has been made to balance these powers with one another, or to form an equilibrium between the one, the few, and the many, for the purpose of enacting and executing equal laws, by common consent, for the general interest, excepting in England.

Shall we conclude, from these melancholy observations, that human nature is incapable of liberty, that no honest equality can be preserved in society, and that such forcible causes are always at work as must reduce all men to a submission to despotism, monarchy, oligarchy, or aristocracy?

By no means.—We have seen one of the first nations in Europe, possessed of ample and fertile territories at home and extensive dominions abroad, of a commerce with the whole world, immense wealth, and the greatest naval power which ever belonged to any nation, which has still preserved the power of the people by the equilibrium we are contending for, by the trial by jury, and by constantly refusing a standing army. The people of England alone, by preserving their share in the legislature, at the expense of the blood of heroes and patriots, have enabled their king to curb the nobility, without giving him a standing army.

After all, let us compare every constitution we have seen with those of the United States of America, and we shall have no reason to blush for our country. On the contrary, we shall feel the strongest motives to fall upon our knees, in gratitude to heaven for having been graciously pleased to give us birth and education in that country, and for having destined us to live under her laws! We shall have reason to exult, if we make our comparison with England and the English constitution. Our people are undoubtedly sovereign—all the landed and other property is in the hands of the citizens—not only their representatives, but their senators and governors, are annually chosen— there are no hereditary titles, honours, offices, or distinctions—the legislative, executive, and judicial powers are carefully separated from each other—the powers of the one, the few, and the many are nicely balanced in the legislatures—trials by jury are preserved in all their glory, and there is no standing army—the *habeas corpus* is in full force—the press is the most free in the world—and where all these circumstances take place, it is unnecessary to add that the laws alone can govern.

From LETTER XXV. [excerpt]
DR. FRANKLIN.

LET US NOW RETURN TO Mr. Turgot's idea of a government consisting in a single assembly.—He tells us our republics are "founded on the equality of all the citizens, and, therefore, 'orders' and 'equilibriums' are unnecessary, and occasion disputes."—But what are we to understand here by equality? Are the citizens to be all of the same age, sex, size, strength, stature, activity, courage, hardiness, industry, patience, ingenuity, wealth, knowledge, fame, wit, temperance, constancy, and wisdom? Was there, or will there ever be, a nation, whose individuals were all equal, in natural and acquired qualities, in virtues, talents, and riches? The answer of all mankind must be in the negative.—It must then be acknowledged, that in every state, in the Massachusetts, for example, there are inequalities which God and nature have planted there, and which no human legislator ever can eradicate. I should have chosen to have mentioned Virginia, as the most ancient state, or indeed any other in the union, rather than the one that gave me birth, if I were not afraid of putting suppositions which may give offence, a liberty which my neighbors will pardon: yet I shall say nothing that is not applicable to all the other twelve.

In this society of Massachusettensions then, there is, it is true, a moral and political equality of rights and duties among all the individuals, and as yet no appearance of artificial inequalities of condition, such as hereditary dignities, titles, magistracies, or legal distinctions; and no established marks, as stars, garters, crosses, or ribbons; there are, nevertheless, inequalities of great moment in the consideration of a legislator, because they have a natural and inevitable influence in society. Let us enumerate some of them:

1. There is an inequality of wealth; some individ-

uals, whether by descent from their ancestors, or from greater skill, industry, and success in business, have estates both in lands and goods of great value; others have no property at all; and of all the rest of society, much the greater number are possessed of wealth, in all the variety of degrees between these extremes; it will easily be conceived that all the rich men will have many of the poor, in the various trades, manufactures, and other occupations in life, dependent upon them for their daily bread: many of smaller fortunes will be in their debt, and in many ways under obligations to them: others, in better circumstances, neither dependent nor in debt, men of letters, men of the learned professions, and others, from acquaintance, conversation, and civilities, will be connected with them and attached to them. Nay, farther, it will not be denied, that among the wisest people that live, there is a degree of admiration, abstracted from all dependence, obligation, expectation, or even acquaintance, which accompanies splendid wealth, insures some respect, and bestows some influence.

2. Birth. Let no man be surprised that this species of inequality is introduced here. Let the page in history be quoted, where any nation, ancient or modern, civilized or savage, is mentioned, among whom no difference was made between the citizens, on account of their extraction. The truth is, that more influence is allowed to this advantage in free republics than in despotic governments, or than would be allowed to it in simple monarchies, if severe laws had not been made from age to age to secure it. The children of illustrious families have generally greater advantages of education, and earlier opportunities to be acquainted with public characters, and informed of public affairs, than those of meaner ones, or even than those in middle life; and what is more than all, an habitual national veneration for their names, and the characters of their ancestors described in history, or coming down by tradition, removes them farther from vulgar jealousy and popular envy, and secures them in some degree the favor, the affection, and respect of the public. Will any man pretend that the name of Andros, and that of

Winthrop, are heard with the same sensations in any village of New England? Is not gratitude the sentiment that attends the latter, and disgust the feeling excited by the former? In the Massachusetts, then, there are persons descended from some of their ancient governors, counsellors, judges, whose fathers, grandfathers, and great-grandfathers, are remembered with esteem by many living, and who are mentioned in history with applause, as benefactors to the country, while there are others who have no such advantage. May we go a step farther—Know thyself, is as useful a precept to nations as to men. Go into every village in New England, and you will find that the office of justice of the peace, and even the place of representative, which has ever depended only on the freest election of the people, have generally descended from generation to generation, in three or four families at most. The present subject is one of those which all men respect, and all men deride. It may be said of this part of our nature, as Pope said of the whole:

Of human nature, wit her worst may write,
We all revere it in our own despite.

If, as Harrington says, the ten commandments
were voted by the people of Israel, and have been
enacted as laws by all other nations; and if we
should presume to say, that nations had a civil
right to repeal them, no nation would think proper
to repeal the fifth, which enjoins honour to parents: if there is a difference between right and
wrong; if any thing can be sacred; if there is one
idea of moral obligation; the decree of nature must
force upon every thinking being and upon every
feeling heart the conviction that honour, affection,
and gratitude are due from children to those who
gave them birth, nurture, and education. The sentiments and affections which naturally arise from
reflecting on the love, the cares, and the blessings
of parents, abstracted from the consideration of
duty, are some of the most forcible and most universal. When religion, law, morals, affection, and
even fashion, thus conspire to fill every mind with
attachment to parents, and to stamp deep upon

the heart their impressions, is it to be expected that men should reverence their parents while they live, and begin to despise or neglect their memories as soon as they are dead? This is in nature impossible. On the contrary, every little unkindness and severity is forgotten, and nothing but endearments remembered with pleasure.

The son of a wise and virtuous father finds the world about him sometimes as much disposed as he himself is, to honour the memory of his father; to congratulate him as the successor to his estate; and frequently to compliment him with elections to the offices he held. A sense of duty, his passions and his interest, thus conspiring to prevail upon him to avail himself of this advantage, he finds a few others in similar circumstances with himself; they naturally associate together, and aid each other. This is a faint sketch of the source and rise of the family spirit: very often the disposition to favor the family is as strong in the town, county, province, or kingdom, as it is in the house itself. The enthusiasm is indeed sometimes wilder, and carries away, like a torrent, all before it.

These observations are not peculiar to any age; we have seen the effects of them in St. Marino, Biscay, and the Grisons, as well as in Poland, and all other countries. Not to mention any notable examples which have lately happened near us, it is not many months since I was witness to a conversation between some citizens of Massachusett's: one was haranguing on the jealousy which a free people ought to entertain of their liberties, and was heard by all the company with pleasure. In less than ten minutes, the conversation turned upon their governor; and the jealous republican was very angry at the opposition to him. "The present governor," says he, "has done us such services, that he ought to rule us, he and his posterity after him, for ever and ever." Where is your jealousy of liberty? demanded the other. "Upon my honour," replies the orator, "I had forgot that; you have caught me in an inconsistency; for I cannot know whether a child of five years old will be a son of liberty or a tyrant." His jealousy was the dictate of his understanding: his confidence and enthusiasm the impulse of his heart.

The pompous trumpery of ensigns, armorials, and escutcheons, are not indeed far advanced in America. Yet there is a more general anxiety to know their originals, in proportion to their numbers, than in any nation of Europe; arising from the easier circumstances and higher spirit of the common people: and there are certain families in every state equally attentive to all the proud frivolities of heraldry. That kind of pride, which looks down on commerce and manufactures as degrading, may, indeed, in many countries of Europe, be a useful and necessary quality in the nobility: it may prevent, in some degree, the whole nation from being entirely delivered up to the spirit of avarice: it may be the cause why honour is preferred by some to money: it may prevent the nobility from becoming too rich, and acquiring too large a proportion of the landed property. In America, it would not only be mischievous, but would expose the highest pretensions of the kind to universal ridicule and contempt. Those other hauteurs, of keeping the commons at a distance, and disdaining to converse with any but a few of a certain race, may in Europe be a favor to the people, by relieving them from a multitude of assiduous attentions and humiliating compliances, which would be troublesome; it may prevent the nobles from caballing with the people, and gaining too much influence with them in elections and otherwise. In America, it would justly excite universal indignation; the vainest of all must be of the people, or be nothing. While every office is equally open to every competitor, and the people must decide upon every pretension to a place in the legislature, that of governor and senator, as well as representative, no such airs will ever be endured. At the same time, it must be acknowledged, that some men must take more pains to deserve and acquire an office than others, and must behave better in it, or they will not hold it.

We cannot presume that a man is good or bad, merely because his father was one or the other; and we should always inform ourselves first, whether the virtues and talents are inherited, before we yield our confidence. Wise men beget fools, and honest men knaves; but these instances, although they may be frequent, are not general. If there is often a likeness in feature and figure, there is generally more in mind and heart, because education contributes to the formation of these as well as nature. The influence of example is very great, and almost universal, especially that of parents over their children. In all countries it has been observed, that vices, as well as virtues, very often run down in families from age to age. Any man may go over in his thoughts the circle of his acquaintance, and he will probably recollect instances of a disposition to mischief, malice, and revenge, descending in certain breeds from grandfather to father and son. A young woman was lately convicted at Paris of a trifling theft, barely within the law which decreed a capital punishment. There were circumstances, too, which greatly alleviated her fault; some things in her behavior that seemed innocent and modest; every spectator, as well as the judges, was affected at the scene, and she was advised to petition for a pardon, as there was no doubt it would be granted. "No," says she, "my grandfather, father, and brother, were all hanged for stealing; it runs in the blood of our family to steal, and be hanged; if I am pardoned now, I shall steal again in a few months more inexcusably: and, therefore, I will be hanged now."— An hereditary passion for the halter is a strong instance, to be sure, and cannot be very common: but something like it too often descends in certain breeds, from generation to generation.

If vice and infamy are thus rendered less odious, by being familiar in a family, by the example of parents and by education, it would be as unhappy as unaccountable, if virtue and honour were not recommended and rendered more amiable to children by the same means.

There are, and always have been, in every state, numbers possessed of some degree of family pride, who have been invariably encouraged, if not flattered in it, by the people. These have most acquaintance, esteem, and friendship with each other, and mutually aid each other's schemes of interest, convenience, and ambition. Fortune, it is true, has more influence than birth; a rich man of an ordinary family and common decorum of conduct, may have greater weight than any family merit commonly confers without it.

3. It will be readily admitted, there are great inequalities of merit, or talents, virtues, services, and, what is of more moment, very often of reputation. Some, in a long course of service in an army, have devoted their time, health, and fortunes, signalized their courage and address, exposed themselves to hardships and dangers, lost their limbs, and shed their blood, for the people. Others have displayed their wisdom, learning, and eloquence in council, and in various other ways acquired the confidence and affection of their fellow-citizens to such a degree, that the public have settled into a kind of habit of following their example and taking their advice.

4. There are a few, in whom all these advantages of birth, fortune, and fame are united.

These sources of inequality, which are common to every people, and can never be altered by any, because they are founded in the constitution of nature; this natural aristocracy among mankind, has been dilated on, because it is a fact essential to be considered in the institution of a government. It forms a body of men which contains the greatest collection of virtues and abilities in a free government, is the brightest ornament and glory of the nation, and may always be made the greatest blessing of society, if it be judiciously managed in the constitution. But if this be not, it is always the most dangerous; nay, it may be added, it never fails to be the destruction of the commonwealth. What shall be done to guard against it? Shall they be all massacred? This experiment has been more than once attempted, and once at least executed. Guy Faux attempted it in England; and a king of Denmark, aided by a popular party, effected it once in Sweden; but it answered no good end. The moment they were dead another aristocracy instantly arose, with equal art and influence, with less delicacy and discretion, if not principle, and behaved more intolerably than the former. The country, for centuries, never recovered from the ruinous consequences of a deed so horrible, that one would think it only to be met with in the history of the kingdom of darkness.

There is but one expedient yet discovered, to avail the society of all the benefits from this body of men, which they are capable of affording, and at the same time, to prevent them from undermining or invading the public liberty; and that is, to throw them all, or at least the most remarkable of them, into one assembly together, in the legislature; to keep all the executive power entirely out of their hands as a body; to erect a first magistrate over them, invested with the whole executive authority; to make them dependent on that executive magistrate for all public executive employments; to give that first magistrate a negative on the legislature, by which he may defend both himself and the people from all their enterprises in the legislature; and to erect on the other side an impregnable barrier against them, in a house of commons, fairly, fully, and adequately representing the people, who shall have the power both of negativing all their attempts at encroachment in the legislature, and of withholding from them and from the crown all supplies, by which they may be paid for their services in executive offices, or even the public service may be carried on to the detriment of the nation.

We have seen, both by reasoning and in experience, what kind of equality is to be found or expected in the simplest people in the world. There is not a city nor a village, any more than a kingdom or a commonwealth, in Europe or America; not a horde, clan, or tribe, among the negroes of Africa, or the savages of North or South America; nor a private club in the world, in which inequalities are not more or less visible. There is, then, a certain degree of weight, which property, family, and merit, will have: if Mr. Turgot had discovered a mode of ascertaining the quantity which they ought to have, and had revealed it to mankind, so that it might be known to every citizen, he would have deserved more of gratitude than is due to all the inventions of philosophers. But, as long as human nature shall have passions and imagination, there is too much reason to fear that these advantages, in many instances, will have more influence than reason and equity can justify.

LETTER XXVI. [excerpt]
DR. PRICE.

Upon these principles, and to establish a method of enacting laws that must of necessity be wise and equal, the people of most of the United States of America agreed upon that division of the legislative power into two houses, the house of representatives and the senate, which have given so much disgust to Mr. Turgot. Harrington will show us equally well the propriety and necessity of the other branch, the governor: but before we proceed to that, it may be worth while to observe the similitude between this passage and some of those sentiments and expressions of Swift, which were quoted in a former letter; and there is in the Idea of a Patriot King, written by his friend, Lord Bolingbroke, a passage to the same purpose, so nobly expressed, that I cannot forbear the pleasure of transcribing it. "It seems to me that, in order to maintain the moral system of the universe at a certain point, far below that of ideal perfection (for we are made capable of conceiving what we are not capable of attaining), it has pleased the Author of Nature to mingle, from time to time, among the societies of men a few, and but a few of those on whom he has been graciously pleased to confer a larger proportion of the ethereal spirit, than in the ordinary course of his providence he bestows on the sons of men. These are they who engross almost the whole reason of the species. Born to direct, to guide, and to preserve, if they retire from the world their splendor accompanies them, and enlightens even the darkness of their retreat. If they take a part in public life, the effect is never indifferent: they either appear the instruments of Divine vengeance, and their course through the world is marked by desolation and oppression, by poverty and servitude; or they are the guardian angels of the country they inhabit, studious to avert the most distant evil, and to procure peace, plenty, and the greatest of human blessings, liberty."

If there is then, in society, such a natural aristocracy as these great writers pretend, and as all history and experience demonstrate, formed partly by genius, partly by birth, and partly by riches, how shall the legislator avail himself of their influence for the equal benefit of the public? and how, on the other hand, shall he prevent them from disturbing the public happiness? I answer, by arranging them all, or at least the most conspicuous of them, together in one assembly, by the name of a senate; by separating them from all pretensions to the executive power, and by controuling, in the legislature, their ambition and avarice, by an assembly of representatives on one side, and by the executive authority on the other. Thus you will have the benefit of their wisdom, without fear of their passions. If among them there are some of Lord Bolingbroke's guardian angels, there will be some of his instruments of Divine vengeance too: the latter will be here restrained by a threefold tie; by the executive power, by the representative assembly, and by their peers in the senate. But if these were all admitted into a single popular assembly, the worst of them might in time obtain the ascendency of all the rest. In such a single assembly, as has been observed before, almost the whole of this aristocracy will make its appearance; being returned members of it by the election of the people. These will be one class. There will be another set of members, of middling rank and circumstances, who will justly value themselves upon their independence, their integrity, and unbiased affection to their country, and will pique themselves upon being under no obligation. But there will be a third class, every one of whom will have his leader among the members of the first class, whose character he will celebrate, and whose voice he will follow; and this party, after a course of time, will be the most numerous. The question then will be, whether this aristocracy in the house will unite or divide? and it is too obvious, that destruction to freedom must be the consequence equally of their union or of their division. If they unite generally in all things, as much as they certainly will in respecting each other's wealth, birth, and parts, and conduct themselves with prudence, they will strengthen themselves by insensible degrees, by playing into each other's hands more